The Ca:

Cookbook

Delicious Cast Iron Skillet Recipes the
Whole Family Loves

BY: Nancy Silverman

COPYRIGHT NOTICES

My Heartfelt Thanks and A Special Reward for Your Purchase!

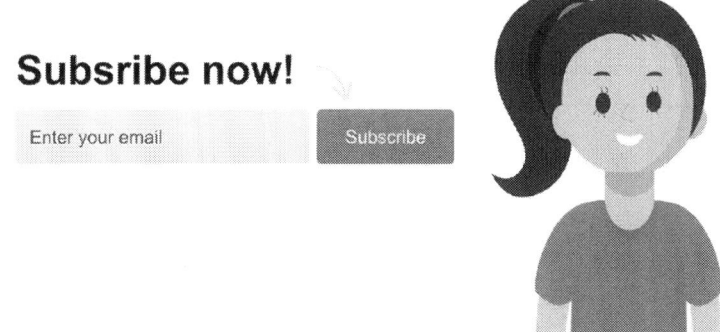

https://nancy.gr8.com

My heartfelt thanks at purchasing my book and I hope you enjoy it! As a special bonus, you will now be eligible to receive books absolutely free on a weekly basis! Get started by entering your email address in the box above to subscribe. A notification will be emailed to you of my free promotions, no purchase necessary! With little effort, you will be eligible for free and discounted books daily. In addition to this amazing gift, a reminder will be sent 1-2 days before the offer expires to remind you not to miss out. Enter now to start enjoying this special offer!

Table of Contents

25 Delicious Cast-Iron Skillet Recipes

||||||||||||||||||||||||||||||||||||||||||||||||||||||||

(1) Skillet Seared Pork Chops

This is one of my favorite recipes, and I know once you get a taste of it, it will become your favorite as well. Serve this with fresh vegetables for the tastiest results.

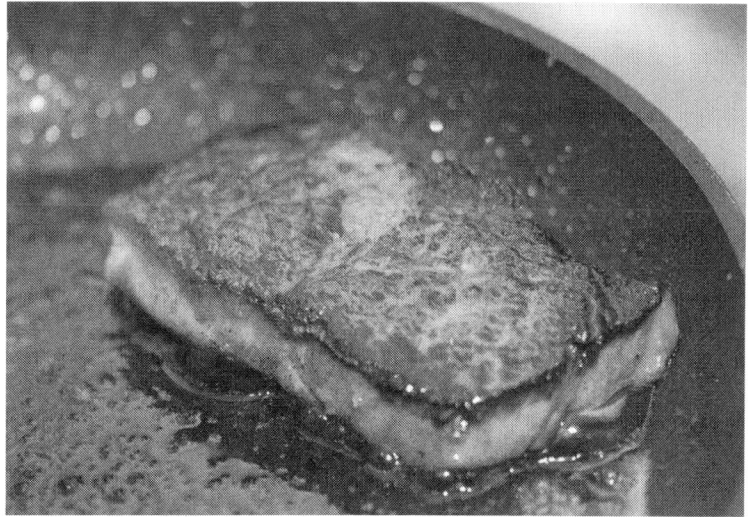

Serving Size: 2 Servings

Preparation Time: 24 Hours

Ingredient List:

- 2, 12 to 16 oz. pork chops, bone in
- 2 tablespoons of salt
- 1 ½ teaspoon of sugar
- Dash of black pepper
- 2 tablespoons of butter
- 1 shallot, thinly sliced
- 2 tablespoons of vegetable oil
- 8 sprigs of thyme, fresh

|||||||||||||||||||||||||||||||||||||||||||||||||||||||

Instructions:

1. Pat the pork chops dry with paper towels.
2. Season the pork chops with the salt and sugar. Cover and place in the fridge to chill for the 8 to 24 hours.
3. Preheat the oven to 250°F.
4. Place the pork chops on a large baking sheet. Place in the oven to bake for 35 minutes. Remove and set aside.
5. In a large, cast-iron skillet, on the high heat, add the oil and, once the oil begins to smoke, add the pork chops. Cook for 2 minutes on both sides before adding the shallots, butter and thyme.
6. Continue to cook for another 1 to 2 minutes, basting the pork chops with the butter as it cooks.
7. Remove and allow to rest for 5 minutes. Serve with the pan sauce drizzled on top.

(2) Cast-Iron Skillet Shepherd's Pie

Here is another great-tasting, cast-iron skillet recipe you can make whenever you need something filling. It is packed-full of beef, healthy vegetables, and topped with mashed potatoes, making it one of the easiest and most delicious skillet recipes you can make for the entire family.

Serving Size: 8 Servings

Preparation Time: 1 Hour and 25 Minutes

Ingredients for the meat:

- 1 tablespoon of extra virgin olive oil
- 1 ¼ lb. of beef, lean and ground
- Dash of salt and black pepper
- 1 onion, chopped
- 1 clove of garlic, minced
- ½ teaspoon of red pepper flakes, crushed
- 2 tablespoons of Worcestershire sauce
- 9 oz. pack of onion soup mix
- 1 cup of beef broth
- 2 cups of mixed frozen vegetables

Ingredients for the mashed potatoes:

- 6 potatoes, peeled and cut into small cubes
- 4 tablespoons of butter, soft
- 2/3 cup of milk, whole
- ¼ cup of parmesan cheese, grated
- Dash of salt and black pepper
- 1 tablespoon of parsley, fresh and chopped

Instructions:

1. Fill a saucepan with salted water and bring to the boil. Add the potatoes and boil for 15 minutes or until soft.

2. In a large, cast-iron skillet, over medium heat, add the oil and, once the oil is hot enough, add the beef and cook for 5 to 10 minutes or until the beef is browned.

3. Add the onions and garlic and cook for 3 to 5 minutes or until the onions are soft.

4. Add the red pepper flakes, Worcestershire sauce, onion soup, and beef broth and bring to a slow boil.

5. Add the frozen vegetables and continue to cook for 5 to 10 minutes or until the vegetables are soft. Remove from the heat and set aside.

6. Drain the potatoes and add them to a large bowl. In the bowl, add the butter and mash them together until smooth. Add the milk, Parmesan cheese, a dash of salt, and black pepper and mash again until smooth.

7. Spread the mashed potatoes over the meat mixture.

8. Place the skillet on a large baking sheet and transfer to the oven to bake for 40 minutes or until golden on the top.

9. Remove and garnish with parsley.

(3) Quick and Easy Pizza Skillet

To kick things off we have a delicious pizza skillet dish that you can make whenever you are craving pizza. Best of all this dish is completely customizable.

Serving Size: 2 to 4 Servings

Preparation Time: 22 Minutes

Ingredient List:

- 3 tablespoons of extra virgin olive oil
- 12 to 16 oz. of pizza dough, fresh
- ¼ cup of tomato sauce
- ½ teaspoon of oregano, fresh
- 4 oz. of mozzarella, fresh and sliced thinly
- Desired toppings

||||||||||||||||||||||||||||||||||||||||||||||||||||||||||||

Instructions:

1. Heat the oven to 450°F and place a large, cast-iron skillet inside.

2. Place the pizza dough on a lightly floured surface and roll it out into a large circle, 10 inches in diameter.

3. Remove the skillet from oven and then add 2 tablespoons of the olive oil, swirling the pan around to coat the bottom.

4. Place the pizza dough into the skillet.

5. Brush the top of the dough with the remaining olive oil and spread the tomato sauce on top. Sprinkle on the oregano and cheese.

6. Place in the oven and bake for 10 to 12 minutes, or until the cheese is brown. Remove and serve immediately.

(4) Butter and Garlic Parmesan Chicken

This is a great-tasting Parmesan chicken recipe to accompany your next Italian-inspired pasta dish. It is incredibly easy to make and delicious.

Serving Size: 3 Servings

Preparation Time: 25 Minutes

Ingredient List:

- 1 ½ lb. of chicken thighs, skin on and deboned
- Dash of salt and black pepper
- 3 tablespoons of butter, fully melted
- 20 cloves of garlic, peeled and smashed
- ¼ cup of white wine
- ¼ cup of water
- Dash of cayenne pepper
- 1 tablespoon of Italian parsley, fresh and chopped
- 1/3 cup of Parmesan cheese

|||||||||||||||||||||||||||||||||||||||||||||||||||||||

Instructions:

1. Season the chicken with a dash of salt and black pepper.

2. In a large, cast-iron skillet, over medium heat, add the butter and, once the butter is melted, add the chicken, with the skin side facing down. Cook for 10 minutes or until golden brown and crispy on all sides. Remove from the skillet and set aside.

3. In the skillet, add the remaining butter and the garlic and cook for 1 minute.

4. Return the chicken to the skillet along with the white wine and water. Stir well and reduce the heat to low, allowing it to simmer for 10 minutes.

5. Season with a dash of cayenne pepper.

6. Continue to cook until the sauce is reduced.

7. Top with the parsley and Parmesan cheese.

8. Transfer to the over and broil for 5 minutes or until the cheese melts. Remove and serve immediately.

(5) Giant, Chocolate-Chip, Cast-Iron Skillet Cookie

If you have a strong sweet tooth that needs to be satisfied, then this is the perfect dish for you to make. This recipe makes such a big cookie, you'll be able to share it will plenty of people.

Serving Size: 6 Servings

Preparation Time: 1 Hour

Ingredient List:

- 2 cups of flour, all-purpose
- 1 teaspoon of baker-style baking soda
- 1 teaspoon of sea salt
- ¾ cup of butter, soft
- ½ cup of cane sugar, organic
- ¾ cup of brown sugar, light and packed
- 1 egg, large
- 2 teaspoons of pure vanilla
- 10 oz. of chocolate chips, semi-sweet

IIIIIIIIIIIIIIIIIIIIIIIIIIIIIIIIIIIIIIIIIIIIIIIIIIIIIIIIII

Instructions:

1. Preheat the oven to 350°F.
2. In a large bowl, add the flour, baking soda, and a dash of salt.
3. In a separate, large bowl, add the butter, sugar, and brown sugar. Beat with an electric mixer for 2 minutes or until the mixture is creamy. Add the egg and vanilla and then beat again to incorporate.
4. Add the flour mixture and beat well.
5. Add the chocolate chips and fold gently to incorporate.
6. Spread the cookie dough in a large cast-iron skillet.
7. Place in the oven to bake for 30 to 40 minutes or until the edges are golden.
8. Remove and allow to cool for 20 minutes before serving.

(6) Cast-Iron Skillet Banana Nut Bread

This is a cast-iron skillet dish you can make for the holiday season. It is sweet and packed-full of a nutty taste that your entire family will be impressed with.

Serving Size: 10 Servings

Preparation Time: 45 Minutes

Ingredient List:

- ½ cup of butter, unsalted, melted and cooled
- 1/3 cup of buttermilk
- 3 bananas, mashed
- 2 eggs, large
- 1 teaspoon of pure vanilla
- 2 cups of flour, all-purpose
- ½ cup of sugar, granulated
- ½ cup of brown sugar, light and packed
- 1 teaspoon of baker-style baking soda
- ½ teaspoon of salt
- 1 cup of pecans, chopped
- ¼ teaspoon of mace, ground
- ¼ teaspoon of allspice
- 1 tablespoon of butter, unsalted

Instructions:

1. Preheat the oven to 350°F.
2. In a medium bowl, add the mashed bananas.
3. Add the buttermilk, butter, vanilla, and eggs and mix well. Set aside.
4. In a small bowl, add the sugar, flour, baking soda, brown sugar, a dash of salt, pecans, mace, and allspice and mix to combine. Add to the buttermilk mixture and stir well until combined.
5. Grease a large, cast-iron skillet with cooking spray and pour in the bread batter.
6. Place in the oven to bake for 35 minutes or until completely baked through.
7. Remove and allow to cool for 5 minutes before serving.

(7) Easy Peach Cobbler

Here is another great-tasting, cast-iron skillet dish you can make when you want something on the sweet side. Make this for a special treat for the entire family to enjoy.

Serving Size: 6 to 8 Servings

Preparation Time: 55 Minutes

Ingredient List:

- 29 oz. can of peaches, sliced and drained
- 2 sticks of butter, melted
- 2 cups of sugar, white
- 2 cups of flour, all-purpose
- 2 cups of milk, whole
- 2 teaspoons of baker-style baking powder

‖‖‖

Instructions:

1. Preheat the oven to 350°F.
2. In a large, cast-iron skillet, add the peaches and pour the butter on top.
3. In a large bowl, add the sugar, flour, milk, and baking powder and stir until a batter forms.
4. Pour the batter over the peaches.
5. Place in the oven to bake for 30 to 45 minutes or until the top is golden. Remove and allow to cool for 10 minutes before serving.

(8) Greek Lemon Chicken Skillet

This is another, great-tasting, cast-iron skillet recipe to make whenever you are craving Greek cuisine. This dish is only made with a few ingredients so it's simple enough for any cook.

Serving Size: 5 Servings

Preparation Time: 45 Minutes

Ingredient List:

- 5 chicken thighs, bone in and with the skin on
- ¼ cup of extra virgin olive oil
- 3 cloves of garlic, minced
- ½ teaspoon of salt
- ¼ teaspoon of black pepper
- 1 teaspoon of oregano, dried
- ¼ teaspoon of red pepper flakes, crushed
- ½ teaspoon of thyme, dried
- 2 lemons, one lemon cut into wedges and the other juices and zested

IIIIIIIIIIIIIIIIIIIIIIIIIIIIIIIIIIIIIIIIIIIIIIIIIIIIIIIIIIIIIII

Instructions:

1. Preheat the oven to 375°F.

2. In a large bowl, add the chicken thighs, olive oil, garlic, oregano, red pepper flakes, thyme, lemon juice, lemon zest, a dash of salt, and black pepper. Stir well to mix.

3. Transfer to a large, cast-iron skillet, making sure the chicken faces skin side up.

4. Scatter the lemon wedges around the chicken.

5. Place in the oven to bake for 40 minutes or until the chicken skin is crispy and brown.

6. Remove and allow to cool for 5 minutes before serving.

(9) Pan-Seared Filet Mignon with Herb Butter

If you ever want to make a dinner that will satisfy and impress your significant other, then this is the perfect dish for you. Serve this dish with some fresh vegetables for the tastiest results.

Serving Size: 4 Servings

Preparation Time: 20 Minutes

Ingredient List:

- 4, 10 oz. tenderloin beef fillets, thick
- 2 tablespoons of extra virgin olive oil
- 2 tablespoons of butter, soft
- Dash of salt and black pepper

Ingredients for the herb butter:

- ½ stick of butter
- 1 tablespoon of rosemary, fresh and chopped
- 1 tablespoon of tarragon, fresh and chopped
- ½ tablespoon of garlic, minced

IIIIIIIIIIIIIIIIIIIIIIIIIIIIIIIIIIIIIIIIIIIIIIIIIIIIIIIIIIIII

Instructions:

1. In a small, microwave-safe bowl add the butter and microwave for 10 seconds or until soft.

2. Add the rosemary, tarragon, and garlic and mix well. Place the butter onto aluminum foil and shape the butter to form a stick. Allow to chill in the fridge for 10 minutes.

3. Preheat the oven to 415°F.

4. Season the beef fillets with a dash of salt and black pepper.

5. In a large cast-iron skillet, over high heat, add the olive oil and butter. Allow to heat for 1 to 2 minutes or until the skillet is searing hot. Add the fillets to the skillet and then sear for 2 minutes on either sides.

6. Transfer the skillet directly to the oven to bake for 6 to 7 minutes. Remove and allow to rest for about 5 minutes.

7. Serve with a piece of herb butter.

(10) Brown Butter and Honey-Garlic Salmon

Here is yet another salmon dish I know you are going to fall in love with. Best of all, this salmon is sweet in taste making it perfect for those with a sweet tooth.

Serving Size: 4 Servings

Preparation Time: 15 Minutes

Ingredient List:

- 4 tablespoons of butter, low-in-fat
- 4 tablespoons of honey
- 1 tablespoon of lemon juice, fresh
- 2 cloves over garlic, minced
- 4 salmon fillets
- Dash of sea salt
- Lemon wedges, fresh and for serving

||||||||||||||||||||||||||||||||||||||||||||||||||||||||

Instructions:

1. Preheat an outdoor grill to medium-high heat.

2. In a large, cast-iron skillet, over medium heat, add the butter and swirl it around the skillet to coat the bottom. Continue to cook until brown in color and nutty in aroma. Set aside some of the butter for serving.

3. Add the honey, lemon juice, and garlic and cook for an additional minute.

4. Add the salmon and sear on all sides for 3 to 4 minutes each or until the salmon is golden.

5. Transfer to the grill and cook for 6 minutes.

6. Remove and serve with a drizzle of the brown butter on top.

(11) Cast-Iron Skillet Chicken Parmesan

This is a great-tasting, cast-iron skillet dish to make whenever you are craving authentic Italian food. Make this any time of the year for a filling dish that everybody will fall in love with.

Serving Size: 4 Servings

Preparation Time: 55 Minutes

Ingredient List:

- 2 chicken breasts, cut into halves
- 1 ½ cups of breadcrumbs
- 1 cup of parmesan cheese, grated + 2 tablespoons extra
- 2 tablespoons of basil, fresh and minced
- 2 eggs, large
- 1 teaspoon of water
- ½ cup of flour, all-purpose
- 1/3 cup of extra virgin olive oil
- 1 ½ cups of tomato sauce
- 8 oz. of mozzarella cheese, fresh and sliced

||||||||||||||||||||||||||||||||||||||||||||||||||||||||||

Instructions:

1. Preheat the oven to 350°F.

2. Cut the chicken breasts into 4 slices and flatten each piece with a rolling pin, until ½ an inch thick.

3. In a small bowl, add the breadcrumbs, ½ a cup of parmesan cheese, and basil. Set aside.

4. In a separate, small bowl, add the water and eggs and whisk well. Add the flour to a medium plate. Set both aside.

5. Coat the chicken in the flour, shaking off the excess, followed by a dip in the egg mixture. Last roll the chicken in the breadcrumbs, coating all sides.

6. In a large cast-iron skillet, over medium-high heat, add the olive oil and, once the oil is hot enough, add the chicken slices. Cook for 2 to 3 minutes on both sides or until golden. Remove and transfer to a large plate.

7. Pour ½ a cup of tomato sauce to the cast-iron skillet. Return the chicken slices to the skillet.

8. Cover the chicken with the remaining sauce and sprinkle the remaining parmesan cheese and mozzarella cheese on top. Sprinkle a touch of basil on top.

9. Place in the oven to bake for 30 minutes. Remove and serve immediately.

(12) Campfire Whiskey BBQ Chicken Skillet

You don't have to keep this recipe for your camping trips, you can make it anywhere and anytime you wish. This is a sweet-tasting chicken dish that I know you won't get enough of.

Serving Size: 6 Servings

Preparation Time: 35 Minutes

Ingredients for the sauce:

- 1 ¼ cups of ketchup
- 1 to 1 ½ teaspoon of hot sauce
- 2 tablespoons of molasses, dark
- 2 tablespoons of Dijon mustard
- 2 tablespoons of whiskey
- 2 tablespoons of Worcestershire sauce
- 1 tablespoon of vinegar, apple cider
- 1 clove of garlic, minced

Ingredients for the chicken:

- 6 chicken legs with thighs, cut into halves
- 1 tablespoon of extra virgin olive oil

IIIIIIIIIIIIIIIIIIIIIIIIIIIIIIIIIIIIIIIIIIIIIIIIIIIIIIIIIIIIIII

Instructions:

1. Preheat an outdoor grill to medium heat.

2. In a medium saucepan, over medium heat, add all the sauce ingredients and whisk to mix. Cover and allow it to simmer for 45 minutes.

3. Place the chicken in a large bowl, drizzle with the olive oil, and toss to coat.

4. Place a cast-iron skillet directly over the grill. Add the chicken and grill for 15 minutes or until golden brown on all sides. Flip and baste with the sauce. Continue to cook for an additional 15 minutes or until completely cooked through.

5. Remove and serve with the remaining barbecue sauce on the side.

(13) Skillet Spinach and Artichoke Dip

If you have always wanted to make your own spinach and artichoke dip from scratch, then this recipe is for you. Serve this with your favorite tortilla chips or homemade bread for the tastiest results.

Serving Size: 4 Servings

Preparation Time: 25 Minutes

Ingredients for the béchamel sauce:

- 4 tablespoons of butter, unsalted
- ½ tablespoon of garlic, minced
- ¼ cup of flour, all-purpose
- 2 cups of milk, whole
- Dash of salt
- Dash of cayenne pepper
- 1 teaspoon of thyme leaves, fresh

Ingredients for the artichoke dip:

- ½ of the béchamel sauce
- ½ cup of gruyere cheese
- ¼ cup of mozzarella cheese, shredded
- 2 to 3 tablespoons of parmesan cheese, grated
- 1 tablespoon of butter, unsalted
- Dash of salt
- 2 cups of spinach, fresh and chopped
- 6 ½ oz. jar of artichoke hearts, drained and chopped
- ¼ cup of mozzarella cheese, shredded

Instructions:

1. In a medium saucepan, over low heat, add the butter and, once the butter is melted, the garlic. Cook for 30 seconds.

2. Add the flour and whisk to mix. Continue to cook for 5 minutes before adding the milk and whisking to combine.

3. Add the thyme leaves, salt, and cayenne pepper and stir well to combine. Allow to cook for 5 to 10 minutes or until it thickens.

4. In a separate, medium saucepan, over medium heat, add ½ of the cooked béchamel sauce, salt, and, once piping hot, add the 3 cheeses and whisk until smooth and creamy.

5. Preheat the oven to broil.

6. In a large, cast-iron skillet, over medium heat, add the butter and, once the butter is melted, add the spinach and artichoke hearts. Stir well and cook for 2 to 3 minutes or until the spinach is wilted.

7. Pour the cheese sauce into the skillet and stir well to mix.

8. Top with the remaining mozzarella cheese.

9. Transfer the skillet to the oven and broil for 5 minutes or until the cheese is brown. Remove and serve immediately.

(14) Cast-Iron Skillet Seared Salmon

This is perhaps the best-tasting salmon recipes you will ever have the pleasure of tasting. It is also incredibly easy to make; even those with no cooking experience can easily put this dish together.

Serving Size: 2 Servings

Preparation Time: 18 Minutes

Ingredient List:

- 16 oz. of salmon, fresh and cut into 2 pieces
- Dash of salt
- ¼ teaspoon of black pepper
- 1 cup of tomatoes, cherry and cut into halves
- 2 tablespoons of tarragon, fresh and chopped
- 1 tablespoon of butter, unsalted

llllllllllllllllllllllllllllllllllllllllllllllllllllllllllll

Instructions:

1. Preheat the oven to 450°F. Grease a large, cast-iron skillet with cooking spray.
2. Spray the salmon fillets with cooking spray and season with a dash of salt and black pepper.
3. In the skillet, over medium-high heat, add the salmon and sear for 1 minute on either side.
4. Add the cherry tomatoes around the salmon and sprinkle the tarragon on top.
5. Add the butter and transfer to the oven to bake for 10 minutes.
6. Remove and serve with a garnish of extra tarragon.

(15) Garlic Parmesan Skillet Rolls

This is a bread recipe you can make to accompany your next Italian-inspired meal or soup. Buttery and easily pulled apart, everybody will be itching to grab a piece.

Serving Size: 16 Servings

Preparation Time: 33 Minutes

Ingredient List:

- 1 can of biscuit dough, jumbo
- 4 tablespoons of butter, unsalted and melted
- 3 cloves of garlic, minced
- ½ teaspoon of oregano, dried
- ½ teaspoon of parsley, fresh and dried
- 2 tablespoons of parmesan cheese, grated

||||||||||||||||||||||||||||||||||||||||||||||||||||||||||||||

Instructions:

1. Preheat the oven to 375°F. Grease a large, cast-iron skillet with cooking spray.
2. Divide each biscuit dough in half and, roll each half into a ball (making about 16 balls), and set aside.
3. In a small bowl, add the butter, garlic, parmesan cheese, oregano, and parsley and mix well.
4. Dip each dough ball into the butter mixture and place each in the greased skillet.
5. Place in the oven to bake for 20 minutes or until golden. Remove and serve immediately.

(16) Skillet Chicken Enchiladas

This is a cast-iron skillet recipe you can make when you are craving authentic Latin food. For the tastiest results, serve these enchiladas with fresh guacamole and a side of sour cream.

Serving Size: 2 to 3 Servings

Preparation Time: 35 Minutes

Ingredient List:

- 2 chicken breasts, boneless, skinless and cut into small pieces
- 2, 10 oz. cans of red enchilada sauce
- 2 cups of Mexican cheese blend, shredded
- 15. 5 oz. can of black beans, rinsed
- 4.5 oz. can of green chilies, chopped
- ¼ of cup of green onions, chopped, + 2 tablespoons for garnish
- 5 burrito tortillas
- 1 tablespoon of extra virgin oil
- 1 teaspoon of cumin
- Dash of salt and black pepper

|||||||||||||||||||||||||||||||||||||||||||||||||||||||||||

Instructions:

1. Preheat the oven to 375°F.

2. In a large, cast-iron skillet, over medium-high heat, add the extra virgin olive oil and once the oil is hot enough, add the chicken, green onions, chilies, cumin, a dash of salt, and black pepper. Cook for 5 to 10 minutes or until the chicken is fully cooked. Transfer the mixture to a large bowl and set aside.

3. Remove the skillet from the heat, add ½ a cup of the enchilada sauce, and set aside.

4. Spread the remaining enchilada sauce into the center of each tortilla. Add some of the chicken, onion mixture, black beans, and ½ of the cheese to each tortilla.

5. Roll the tortillas tightly and place in the cast-iron skillet with the seam side facing down.

6. Sprinkle the remaining cheese on top.

7. Place in the oven to bake for 20 to 25 minutes.

8. Remove and garnish with the green onions before serving.

(17) Cast-Iron Skillet Scalloped Potatoes

These delicious, cheesy potatoes go perfectly with almost any dish. Smothered in plenty of cheese, I know this is one dish that you won't be able to get enough of.

Serving Size: 4 Servings

Preparation Time: 1 Hour and 30 Minutes

Ingredient List:

- 6 Yukon gold potatoes, peeled and sliced
- 3 tablespoons of butter, unsalted
- 3 tablespoons of flour, all-purpose
- 1 ½ cups of milk, whole
- 1 ½ to 2 cups of gruyere cheese, shredded
- 2 cloves of garlic, minced
- 1 sprig of thyme, fresh
- Dash of salt and black pepper

||||||||||||||||||||||||||||||||||||||||||||||||||||||||||

Instructions:

1. Preheat your oven to 400°F.

2. In a large, cast-iron skillet, over medium heat, add the butter and reduce the heat to low. Once the butter is melted, add the flour and cook, whisking, for 30 seconds.

3. Add the garlic, thyme, a dash of salt, black pepper, and milk and whisk until smooth. Remove from the heat and transfer the mixture to a medium bowl.

4. Arrange the sliced potatoes in the skillet, overlapping each other, and season with a dash of salt and black pepper.

5. Pour the milk mixture over the potatoes and cover with the gruyere cheese.

6. Cover with aluminum foil and place in the oven to bake for 1 hour. Remove the foil and then continue to bake for 10 minutes or until the top is gold.

7. Remove and allow to cool for 10-15 minutes before serving.

(18) Cast-Iron Skillet Chicken with Bacon and White Wine Sauce

This is a great-tasting, cast-iron skillet chicken dish that is perfect for when you are looking to impress your friends and family. Made with crunchy bacon and smothered in a delicious white wine sauce, this dish is to die for.

Serving Size: 8 Servings

Preparation Time: 1 Hour

Ingredient List:

- 3 slices of bacon, chopped into small cubes
- ½ cup of flour, whole wheat
- Dash of salt and black pepper
- 2 teaspoons of herbs de Provence
- 1 ½ to 2 lb. of chicken thighs, with skin
- 1 to 2 tablespoons of extra virgin olive oil
- 2 shallots, thinly sliced
- ½ cup of white wine, dry
- 1 cup of chicken stock
- Parsley, fresh and for garnish

llllllllllllllllllllllllllllllllllllllllllllllllllllll

Instructions:

1. Preheat the oven to 350°F.

2. In a large, cast-iron skillet, over medium heat, Add the bacon and cook for 5 to 6 minutes. Remove set aside to drain, reserving the bacon grease in the skillet.

3. To a shallow plate, add the flour, herbs de Provence, salt, and black pepper. Dredge the chicken on either side until coated. Add the chicken and remaining flour mixture to the skillet and fry for 5 to 10 minutes or until golden. Remove and set aside.

4. Add the extra virgin olive oil to the skillet and, once the oil is hot enough, add the shallots and cook for 5 to 10 minutes or until soft. Add the white wine, deglaze the skillet, and add the chicken stock. Cook for 10 minutes or until the mixture has reduced.

5. Return the chicken and bacon to the skillet.

6. Place in the oven to bake for 40 minutes, basting the chicken with the sauce occasionally.

7. Remove and serve immediately.

(19) Hasselback Potatoes with Roasted Garlic

Here is another potato recipe you can serve when you want to serve an easy and delicious side dish. This is a great dish to accompany any meat entrée you may prepare.

Serving Size: 6 Servings

Preparation Time: 1 Hour and 45 Minutes

Ingredient List:

- Splash of extra virgin olive oil
- 6 red potatoes, large
- 6 cloves of garlic, peeled and minced
- 1 teaspoon of Italian seasoning
- Dash of salt and black pepper
- ½ cup of butter, cut into small cubes
- ¼ cup of parmesan cheese, shredded

|||||||||||||||||||||||||||||||||||||||||||||||||||||||||||||

Instructions:

1. Preheat the oven to 375°F. Grease a large, cast-iron skillet with olive oil.

2. Using a mandolin, slice the potatoes thinly and place in the skillet vertically.

3. Sprinkle the garlic, Italian seasoning, salt, pepper, and the cubes of butter on the potatoes.

4. Cover with aluminum foil and place in the oven to bake for 1 hour.

5. Remove the foil and continue to bake for 20 minutes or until crispy. Remove and serve immediately.

(20) Caramelized Chicken and Vegetable Skillet

This is a great cast iron skillet recipe to make on a weekend whenever you want to treat yourself to something special. Fill with caramelized onions, I know this is a dish you are going to fall in love with.

Serving Size: 4 Servings

Preparation Time: 50 Minutes

Ingredient List:

- 2 chicken breasts, boneless and skinless
- 3 tablespoons of butter, organic
- 1 tablespoon of extra virgin olive oil
- 2 cloves of garlic, minced
- 1 tablespoon of parmesan cheese, grated
- ½ an onion, thinly sliced
- 2 zucchinis, fresh and chopped
- 1 cup of cauliflower, fresh and chopped
- 3 carrots, fresh and sliced thinly
- 2 tablespoons of cilantro, fresh and chopped
- 1 teaspoon of paprika, powdered
- ½ teaspoon of salt
- ¼ teaspoon of black pepper
- ½ of a lemon, juice only
- ½ cup of water

IIIIIIIIIIIIIIIIIIIIIIIIIIIIIIIIIIIIIIIIIIIIIIIIIIIIIIIIII

Instructions:

1. Preheat the oven to 400°F.
2. In a large, cast-iron skillet, over medium heat, add the onion, chicken breasts, and extra virgin olive oil. Cook the chicken for 2 minutes on either side before adding the paprika and cilantro.
3. Remove the skillet from heat.
4. Add the zucchini, cauliflower, and carrots, tossing well.
5. In a medium bowl, add the butter and melt it in the microwave.
6. Add the lemon juice, parmesan cheese, garlic, a dash of salt, black pepper, and water. Whisk until smooth and add it to the skillet.
7. Place the skillet in the oven to bake for 40 minutes.
8. Remove and serve with a drizzling of extra virgin olive oil on top.

(21) Cast-Iron Skillet Cornbread

This is a great-tasting, cast-iron skillet dish to serve during the Thanksgiving holiday. For the tastiest results serve this bread with honey and butter.

Serving Size: 8 Servings

Preparation Time: 22 Minutes

Ingredient List:

- 1 cup of flour, all-purpose
- 1 cup of cornmeal, yellow
- 1 tablespoon of baker-style baking powder
- ½ teaspoon of salt
- 1 cup of milk, whole
- 1 egg, large and beaten
- 5 tablespoons of vegetable oil

||||||||||||||||||||||||||||||||||||||||||||||||||||||||||||

Instructions:

1. Preheat the oven to 400°F.
2. In a large bowl, add the flour, cornmeal, baking powder, and a dash of salt. Set aside.
3. In a medium bowl, add the egg and milk and whisk well. Add the vegetable oil and whisk again to mix.
4. Pour the egg mixture into the flour mixture and stir well to mix. Pour this mixture into the skillet.
5. Place in the oven to bake for 20 minutes, or until golden brown and completely cooked through. Remove and serve immediately.

(22) Homemade, Rosemary Focaccia Bread

This is a homemade focaccia bread recipe that you can make with relative ease. Soft and chewy on the inside, this bread is perfect when used for your favorite sandwiches.

Serving Size: 4 Servings

Preparation Time: 1 Hour and 55 Minutes

Ingredient List:

- 1 cup of water, lukewarm
- 1 envelope of yeast
- 2 cups of wheat flour, evenly divided
- 1 cup of flour, all-purpose
- 1 teaspoon of salt
- ¼ cup of rosemary, fresh and evenly divided
- Pinch of sea salt, for garnish

|||||||||||||||||||||||||||||||||||||||||||||||||||||||

Instructions:

1. Preheat the oven to 400°F. Grease two, medium, cast-iron skillets with extra virgin olive oil.
2. Using an electric mixer fitted with dough hooks, add the lukewarm water and yeast, stirring well by hand until the yeast dissolves.
3. Add the flours and mix on low until well mixed.
4. Cover and allow to rise for 30 minutes.
5. Add the extra virgin olive oil, a dash of salt, and ½ of the rosemary, mixing until combined.
6. Knead the dough on a floured surface until smooth. Shape the dough into a ball and divide it in two.
7. Place each dough ball into separate skillets, cover again, and set aside to rise for 30 minutes.
8. Brush each loaf with olive oil and sprinkle the remaining rosemary on top.
9. Slice an X in each loaf and sprinkle with the sea salt.
10. Place in the oven to bake for 25 minutes or until it is golden brown. Remove from the oven, brush with more olive oil and allow them to cool for 5 minutes before serving.

(23) Fresh Broccolini, Chicken Sausage, and Orzo

If you are looking for an easy dinner to put together, then this is the perfect recipe for you. It makes enough to leave two people feeling full and satisfied.

Serving Size: 4 Servings

Preparation Time: 30 Minutes

Ingredient List:

- 2 tablespoons of extra virgin olive oil
- 8 oz. of Italian chicken sausage, cooked and cut into rounds
- 2 bunches of broccolini, chopped
- Dash of salt and black pepper
- 2 cloves of garlic, minced
- 1 cup of orzo pasta
- 2 ½ cups of chicken broth, low in sodium
- ½ cup of parmesan, grated and extra for serving

IIIIIIIIIIIIIIIIIIIIIIIIIIIIIIIIIIIIIIIIIIIIIIIIIIIIIIIIII

Instructions:

1. In a large cast-iron skillet, over the medium-high heat, pour in the oil and, once the oil is hot enough, add the Italian chicken sausage. Cook for 3 to 4 minutes on both sides or until browned.

2. Add the broccolini, a dash of salt, and black pepper and continue to cook for 5 minutes or until bright green.

3. Add the orzo and garlic and continue to cook for an additional minute.

4. Pour in the chicken broth and bring to a boil. Cover and lower the heat to a low simmer. Cook for 10 minutes or until the pasta is soft.

5. Uncover and continue to simmer for an additional minute before adding in the parmesan cheese.

6. Remove from the heat and serve.

(24) Cast-Iron Chicken Pot-Pie

This is the perfect dish to make during National Great American Pot Pie Day, especially when you are craving some old-school comfort food. Make this during the fall season when the weather starts getting cold.

Serving Size: 4 Servings

Preparation Time: 25 Minutes

Ingredient List:

- 16 oz. rotisserie chicken, shredded
- 8 oz. can of mixed vegetables, drained
- 8 oz. can of cream of chicken soup
- Dash of salt and black pepper
- 1 bunch of parsley, fresh and chopped
- 1 container of buttermilk biscuits

‖‖

Instructions:

1. Preheat the oven to 425°F. Grease a large, cast-iron skillet with cooking spray.
2. In a large bowl, add the rotisserie chicken and the vegetables
3. Add the cream of chicken soup and stir well to mix.
4. Season with a dash of salt and black pepper.
5. Pour the mixture into the greased skillet, levelling out the mixture with the back of a spoon.
6. Layer the biscuits on top of the mixture.
7. Place in the oven to bake for 20 minutes.
8. Remove and garnish with parsley. Serve immediately.

(25) Baked Macaroni and Cheese

This is a dish you can make whenever you are looking to satisfy those picky eaters in your household. It is so delicious, nobody will be able to resist it.

Serving Size: 6 Servings

Preparation Time: 55 Minutes

Ingredient List:

- 1 ½ cups of elbow macaroni
- 3 tablespoons of butter
- 3 tablespoons of flour, all-purpose
- 2 cups of milk, whole
- ½ teaspoon of salt
- ½ teaspoon of black pepper
- 2 cups of sharp cheddar cheese, shredded

IIIIIIIIIIIIIIIIIIIIIIIIIIIIIIIIIIIIIIIIIIIIIIIIIIIIIIIII

Instructions:

1. Preheat the oven to 350°F.

2. Fill a large pot with salted water and bring to a boil. Cook for 8 to 10 minutes or until the pasta is soft.

3. In a large, cast-iron skillet, over medium-high heat, add the butter and, once melted, the flour. Cook, while whisking, for 1 to 2 minutes or until the mixture is brown.

4. Add the milk and whisk until smooth. Cook for 5 minutes or until it thickens.

5. Add the cheese and continue to cook, while whisking, for an additional minute or until smooth.

6. Drain the pasta and add it to the sauce, tossing to mix.

7. Remove from the heat and transfer to the oven to bake for 40 to 45 minutes or until brown. Remove and serve immediately.

About the Author

Nancy Silverman is an accomplished chef from Essex, Vermont. Armed with her degree in Nutrition and Food Sciences from the University of Vermont, Nancy has excelled at creating e-books that contain healthy and delicious meals that anyone can make and everyone can enjoy. She improved her cooking skills at the New England Culinary Institute in Montpelier Vermont and she has been working at perfecting her culinary style since graduation. She claims that her life's work is always a work in progress and she only hopes to be an inspiration to aspiring chefs everywhere.

Her greatest joy is cooking in her modern kitchen with her family and creating inspiring and delicious meals. She often says that she has perfected her signature dishes based on her family's critique of each and every one.

Nancy has her own catering company and has also been fortunate enough to be head chef at some of Vermont's most exclusive restaurants. When a friend suggested she share some of her outstanding signature dishes, she decided to add cookbook author to her repertoire of personal achievements. Being a technological savvy woman, she felt the e-book realm would be a better fit and soon she had her first cookbook available online. As of today, Nancy has sold over 1,000 e-books and has shared her culinary experiences and brilliant recipes with people from all over the world! She plans on expanding into self-help books and dietary cookbooks, so stayed tuned!

Author's Afterthoughts

Thank you for making the decision to invest in one of my cookbooks! I cherish all my readers and hope you find joy in preparing these meals as I have.

There are so many books available and I am truly grateful that you decided to buy this one and follow it from beginning to end.

I love hearing from my readers on what they thought of this book and any value they received from reading it. As a personal favor, I would appreciate any feedback you can give in the form of a review on Amazon and please be honest! This kind of support will help others make an informed choice on and will help me tremendously in producing the best quality books possible.

My most heartfelt thanks,

Nancy Silverman

If you're interested in more of my books, be sure to follow my author page on Amazon (can be found on the link Bellow) or scan the QR-Code.

https://www.amazon.com/author/nancy-silverman

Printed in Great Britain
by Amazon

73323425R00050